TEXAS
IN COLOR

TEXAS
in Color

TEXT BY
Evelyn Oppenheimer

HASTINGS HOUSE · PUBLISHERS
New York 10016

ACKNOWLEDGEMENTS

In a book such as this, the interested help and cooperation of a number of persons are to be most gratefully acknowledged. As photographic art consultants, thanks are due to the Texas Highway Department, specifically Mr. Tom H. Taylor, Director of Travel and Information; my appreciation too goes to Wanda Brown, Kenneth Brown, Mick Weisberg, F. L. "Bub" Thompson, Clint Grant, the Southwest Scene Magazine of the *Dallas Morning News*, Bill Rhew and Palo Duro Canyon State Park. Special thanks go to Dr. Jenny Lind Porter for permission to quote from her *Siege of the Alamo*. For manuscript typing I am indebted to Mallya Dean Billingsley and for editorial expertise to Harry Hansen and Walter Frese of Hastings House.

PUBLISHED 1971 BY HASTINGS HOUSE, PUBLISHERS, INC.

Third printing, February 1976

Fourth printing, August, 1977

Published simultaneously in Canada by
Saunders, of Toronto, Ltd., Don Mills, Ontario

Library of Congress Catalog Card Number: 79–152808
ISBN 8038–7108–2

Printed and bound in Hong Kong by Mandarin Publishers Limited

CONTENTS

6

I

THIS is not a book of history, though history is in it. Nor is it a guidebook, though hopefully it may beckon you to some 65,335 miles of highways and their exits onto roads that lead to special interests and scenic beauty.

In fact, if this were not an age of ruthless realism, one might call these pages an open love-letter to all five points of the Lone Star State, for in Texas there is still room for romance.

Instead, and if compelled to classification, let us call it a collection of impressions within the necessary limitations of a montage for an image in words and pictures of one of the biggest and most vital parts of the great body of America, a part that adds muscle and strength to the heart of America.

Texas is many things to many people and always has been: escape, refuge, *Lebensraum*, adventure, opportunity, space for man to build what is in him to build, space for man to dream what is in him to dream, wilderness for peace and privacy. Men and women came into its vastness and incredible variety of geography to search for riches or to get lost and find themselves. Many still come for the same reasons, though they use other words.

Tejas, evolving under its six flags of Spain, France, Mexico, the Republic of Texas, the Confederate States of America, and the United States of America, has had a history unique among American states. The effect has rubbed off on the people, not only on the descendants of the oldtimers but also on the new-comers. The result is a flair, a style, an *esprit de corps*. The effect is a pride that can be either conscious or unconscious, offensive or attractive.

What is the reason for this pride? Other regions have great and old traditions, yes, but long before any Pilgrim set foot on the coast of New England there were Europeans on Texas land.

In fact, when the world's most famous protestor, Martin Luther, nailed his 95 theses of questions and exceptions on a church-door in Germany, men of the Old World had already come to Texas. The year was 1519, and they were Spaniards led by Alonzo Alvarez de Pineda for the glory of His Catholic Majesty and Holy Church and also the compulsion to find that water route to India which Columbus had missed 27 years before. They explored and mapped the Gulf coast of Texas and returned with another expedition several years later. Then in 1528 Cabeza de Vaca and his men were shipwrecked in the Galveston Island area, and it was the stories of golden cities of treasure, which they reported hearing about from the native Indians, that generated the Coronado exploration and the many more from New Spain after that. And so we see that the first tall tales of

8

Texas evidently came from the Indian population, which seemed to have had immediate comprehension of the white man's weakness.

Greed, however, has its own strength for survival and conquest. Never had a European seen so much open space. Nor did it ever occur to any of them, Spanish or later French, to question his right to claim all that his eyes could see, plus the vision of his imagination. The priority of the Indian tribes for thousands of years was never considered except as God-given material for conversion and mission-building labor.

The French arrival was in 1685 in the person of the famed explorer Rene Robert Cavelier, Sieur de la Salle, who had already claimed the Mississippi for France. He was planning to establish a colony at the mouth of the great river when his fleet-ship *Amiable* was blown into Matagorda Bay instead and wrecked there. The result was that he had his men erect Fort St. Louis as flagpole for the fleur-de-lys. Whether by accident of storm or in his ambition to compete with Spanish claims, La Salle was ill-fated. He tried to lead some of his men back to the Mississippi, but in rebellion against his leadership or possibly from some motive of personal hatred they murdered him. Just where that Texas wilderness drama took place in 1687 is not known, but the town of Navasota in south central Texas has a statue of him. By coincidence the site is near what was to be the first capital of Texas as a republic, Washington-on-Brazos, two centuries later.

However, in the early 1700's Governor Cadillac of Louisiana also had his eye on Texas for France and sent his agent, Captain Louis de Saint Denis, to a Spanish colony on the Rio Grande.

The excuse was to discuss trade, but the Spaniards were dismayed that a Frenchman could cross Texas to what is now Eagle Pass and not be challenged. They put him in jail, but more important they were spurred to activate their claim to this land and begin to establish missions and settlements all the way into Louisiana.

There were no more French colonies and Cadillac's dream was ended, except to continue in the name of a twentieth century automobile which is rather well represented in Texas.

As for Captain Saint Denis, he did what any astute Frenchman would have done. He married the Spanish commandant's granddaughter and got out of jail very pleasantly.

II

AFTER Mexico won its independence from Spain in 1821, Texas became a state in the new Republic of Mexico. In Mexico City the complexity of government had to be learned too fast for the *mañana* temperament of its people, and the problem of a colonial province as far away and vast as Texas was not easily handled. Texas was being settled more by variously led groups of Anglo-Americans than by Mexicans. The Americans compared the Mexican definition of freedom with that in the United States and found a distasteful discrepancy. The new colonists (more often referred to as filibusters) missed religious freedom and the right to trial by jury. Religion was not of primary concern on that early frontier and neither was law, but the theory of civil rights offered as good a cause then as now.

The colonizing situation and opportunity in Texas was further complicated by the dangling confusions which resulted from the Louisiana Purchase in 1803. There were such uncertainties about the boundary line between the United States and Texas that John Quincy Adams and his Secretary of State Henry Clay questioned the Treaty of 1819, which was the United States disclaimer to Texas. In fact in 1825 Clay and Adams tried to buy Texas from Mexico for a million dollars.

It was easy to enter Texas from Louisiana, U.S.A. One simply crossed the Sabine River, which was a well-behaved little river where the catfish presented no navigational problem.

And so they came—the adventurer, the man who posted the G.T.T. (Gone to Texas) sign on his door in a hurry to escape the sheriff; the American with something in his blood to make him move to a new frontier, new challenge and chance. The Anglo, conditioned to independence and individualism, confronted the Latin American, born to tradition. They spoke a different language in more ways than one.

In 1821, the year when Mexico threw over 300 years of Spanish rule, there were three centers of about 7,000 population in Texas between the Sabine and the Rio Grande at San Antonio, Goliad and Nacogdoches. That was when young Stephen F. Austin implemented the dream of his late father Moses Austin in Missouri by going to San Antonio and Mexico City for official permission to bring in 300 families as colonists to Texas—the "Old Three Hundred".

He settled them at Columbus on the Colorado River and Washington on the Brazos. He insisted on moral character, hard work, and complete cooperation with the Mexican government. Living conditions were primitive, but Austin's colony flourished and increased to over 5,000 men and women as more than 1,000 land grants were issued to him during the next decade.

Other men followed then to lead more colonists into the new land, men such as Ben Milam, David Burnet, General James Wilkinson, and Sterling Robertson. There were even a few Mexican leaders—Lorenzo de Zavala and Martin de Leon. Senor de Leon settled Victoria on the Guadalupe River. By 1836 the total population in Texas shot up to almost 50,000.

The majority of these pioneers were American. It was natural that trade went overland to the United States or through the port at Galveston to New Orleans. After all, Mexico City was 800 miles away across nothing but wilderness. Little commercial profit came to Mexico from Texas.

In addition there was trouble, notably at Nacogdoches in 1826. Hayden Edwards had settled a colony there beside a much older Mexican colony. Conflict developed and Edwards proclaimed an independent Republic of Fredonia. Of course Mexico put a stop to that. In 1830 it enacted a law forbidding any more colonization from the United States. But enactment and enforcement of law are very different things, as Mexico learned.

Texas cotton farmers and Mexican soldiers began fighting at Anahuac and Velasco. Texans held conventions at San Felipe in 1832 and 1833 to request a number of changes in Mexican constitutional law effecting Texas, and Stephen Austin went to Mexico City to represent the cause. There he was put in prison, and this injustice strained relations even more.

Strife-torn Mexico was under the dictatorship of a man too quickly risen to power, Santa Anna, and Texas had a new breed of leadership evolving for more aggressive action. Sam Houston, "The Raven", had crossed the Red River from the north and come to Texas. A veteran of Tennessee politics, close friend of President Andrew Jackson, a military man and adopted son of the Cherokee Indians. Sam Houston was a powerful personality who seemed to have been shaped by destiny for this time and place in history.

There were other men of stature on the scene—William Barret Travis, Jim Bowie, James W. Fannin Jr., David Crockett James Bonham. . . . The list could be very long indeed. Activists all of them.

The Texas Revolution gathered momentum and a provisional government was set up. From the United States came volunteers lured by the promise of bounties of land.

In December, 1835, the Texans defeated a Mexican army and took San Antonio and considered the war ended. But they reckoned without the swashbuckling Santa Anna who stormed into Texas with another army and the threat to "plant the Mexican flag in Washington, D.C.".

From then on the dramatic story has been told by historians, novelists, poets, scenarists—the heroic story of Goliad, the Alamo, San Jacinto.

III

HISTORY has always tended to footnote the part played by women in war, perhaps because their contributions have always stemmed from the weakness in men. So too at San Jacinto there was such a woman, and it is time to escort her out of the cramped quarters of a footnote.

The Texans owe much of their success on that battlefield to this girl, a mulatto girl who inspired the song, "The Yellow Rose of Texas". If at first she was legend, the facts have come to the surface, thanks to the interest and research of popular historian Frank X. Tolbert and Prof. Martha Anne Turner of Sam Houston State University at Huntsville, Texas.

Emily was her name, and she was a bond servant of Colonel James Morgan of Morgan's Point, a Philadelphian who had come to Texas and converted his slaves into indentured servants. When General Santa Anna raided Morgan's Point, his experienced eye selected Emily as a personal prize.

Later when English anthropologist William Bollaert visited

Colonel Morgan on a tour of the new republic, he added a foot-note in the book he wrote about his travels, and the footnote was the story that Morgan had told him, as Emily had reported it on her return home.

Santa Anna had been so engrossed in entertaining her in his tent that he did not choose to hear the cry of warning from his men "The enemy come!" Expertly Emily prolonged the enter-tainment so that the general was too late in attending to his military duties of leadership. There was only time to try to escape the Texans.

In the archives of the University of Texas Library at Austin is a very old handwritten copy of the song, which was published in New York in 1858. Then in 1955 a copyright was recorded for an adaptation that Mitch Miller revived on television. The song for Emily, in its earliest version:

> There's a Yellow Rose in Texas
> That I'm going to see
> No other darky knows her
> No one only me.
>
> She's the sweetest rose of color
> This darky ever knew
> Her eyes are bright as diamonds
> They sparkle like the dew.
>
> We will play the banjo gaily
> And will sing the song of yore
> And the Yellow Rose of Texas
> Shall be mine for evermore!

The result of the battle of San Jacinto was the establishment of the Republic of Texas, a nation for ten years recognized by the

United States and by such major governments in Europe as England, France, and Holland. But it was never recognized by Mexico, which continued to threaten invasion. That threat on the border was handled by the men to become famous as the Texas Rangers.

Sam Houston was the first nationally elected President. Aware that the new nation had land as its only resource, he favored annexation to the United States. With over 100,000 people in the Republic of Texas by 1846, some from the South with their slaves, others from the Midwest, North and Eastern United States, thinking was divided on the slavery issue. The annexation question was edged with political difficulties in both Austin and Washington, D.C. Even so, in 1846 Texas became the 28th state in the Union and the only one to enter by treaty. In addition there were several special provisions. Among them for example, it was provided that public lands were never to be surrendered to the Federal government, and that whenever Texas so desired, it could divide itself into as many as five states.

Annexation brought on another war with Mexico, and that led to the American acquisition of another vast amount of land from the Rio Grande to the Pacific.

Then came the Civil War and Texas joined the Confederacy. Governor Houston was violently opposed to this and he was removed from office. He lived, however, to see that his judgment had held wisdom, for though Texas saw little military action during the war, it got all the adverse effects of the Reconstruction period in radicalism and outlawry.

Prosperity came with movement westward into the great

plains and Panhandle, where cattle could roam by the millions. Then the railroads followed the ranchers, and people and capital poured into the new state.

IV

THE twentieth century opened richly in Texas, not only with agriculture and livestock but industry and the sensational discovery of oil. Texas has led all other states in production of petroleum and natural gas and the multiple by-products and derivatives. Lone Star banks became financial powers regionally and nationally. Urbanization mushroomed as towns became cities and the cities grew into today's metropolitan complexes of manufacturing, distribution and jobbing.

But cities anywhere seldom capture and reflect the charm or flavor of their area's history or geography. A few do, notably New Orleans and San Francisco. In Texas, San Antonio does so with its missions and winding little river.

True, the cities in Texas have the major universities and colleges: Rice University and the University of Houston at Houston, Texas Technological at Lubbock, the University of Texas at Austin with its branches in El Paso, Dallas, Houston, and midway between Dallas and Fort Worth in Arlington; Texas

Christian University at Fort Worth, North Texas State University and Texas Women's University at Denton in the Dallas-Fort Worth region; Baylor University in Waco, Southern Methodist University, the University of Dallas and Bishop College in Dallas. Texas A. & M. University is an exception for its small town location at College Station.

True, too, the cities have the core of culture in their fine symphony orchestras in Houston, Dallas, San Antonio, Fort Worth, Corpus Christi, Amarillo, Midland-Odessa, El Paso, Lubbock, Wichita Falls, Tyler, Beaumont, Austin, San Angelo, and Waco that attract the world's outstanding guest conductors. Opera and ballet companies of high merit and quality also have drawn the best of the old and new stars of America and from abroad to the annual productions in Dallas, Houston, Fort Worth, San Antonio, for example, and frequently offer American debuts for European artists, as has happened in Dallas.

Theater has come alive in Texas at the famed Alley Theater in Houston, Theater Three and the Theater Center in Dallas, and many highly successful university theaters and Little Theaters in other cities.

Back of all this cultural growth has been the cumulative force of women's clubs, their demand for the arts to balance the business interests of their men and the need of their children, as well as their own social life and personal hungers in a land where distances once were isolating. From a few dozen study clubs of small membership but dedicated interest in the classics of Shakespeare, Browning and Bronte, have grown thousands of clubs in every town and city where women want to hear new books and plays reviewed and discussed.

Their pressure also has been largely responsible for the development of libraries, for when a Texan sweeps off his Stetson to a lady, his hand comes out of his pocket. Almost 900 libraries, public, college and special, have been established. The movement goes back to the Republic days of 1839, when $10,000 was appropriated for the first library, though only an 18-volume Edinburgh Encyclopedia was actually purchased.

Outstanding is the new world-famed Humanities Research Center at the University of Texas, with its aggressive collecting of a library of first editions and original manuscripts of twentieth century English and American literature, which has become the envy of university libraries where foresight and Texas-size funds did not concentrate on the literary treasure in our own time. Notable is the wealth of incunabula fast accumulating in the collections of Bridwell Library, located on the campus at Southern Methodist University, which features the largest amount of 15th-century printing east of the Huntington Library in California and west of the Philadelphia Free Public Library. World-famous is the Robert and Elizabeth Barrett Browning Collection in the library at Baylor University in Waco.

Literature itself was originally created directly out of the inspiration of Texas history and the drama of its people and geography. Space was the setting that offered solitude and thought. People offered plot and characterization and folklore.

The first Texas writers to gain national recognition—J. Frank Dobie, Walter Prescott Webb, Roy Bedicheck, Thomas Vernor

Smith, were men who taught and wrote of the worlds of nature, history, folklore, philosophy.

Texan too, for the crucial years in his life, was William Sydney Porter, better known as the short story master O. Henry, who lived in Austin, San Antonio, and Houston, and did some of his earliest writing there.

A classic example of contribution to regional literature of more than regional interest was the dramatic story of the famed King Ranch by Tom Lea, artist-author of El Paso, with special typography executed by Carl Hertzog, also of El Paso.

Another Texas distinction is in the field of lexicography with the work of Ramon F. Adams and his dictionary of western words.

One of the best literary developments in recent years in Texas is that novelists of quality have appeared to add the desirable balance of good fiction. A notable example is William Humphrey, who writes out of his roots in East Texas.

A healthy sign of expansion entirely apart from regional literature is the scholarship of Frances Mossiker in books on 17th and 18th century France.

Few are the major publishers in America today who do not have at least one Texas author on their lists, as new writers on every contemporary subject and interest continue to break through new ground and follow paths not known to the older generation of writers.

Flourishing for many years has been the Poetry Society of Texas, with a large and active membership of many widely published and award-winning poets.

In pictorial art Texas has related itself generally to the

Southwest and the mainstream of the art colonies of New Mexico, where reaction to the scenic holds both realism and symbolism in what is created.

Art galleries and museums have become distinguished in all the major cities, especially the Amon Carter Museum of Western Art in Fort Worth, and the Dallas Museum of Fine Arts. Well under way is the project at Texas Technological University in Lubbock for a 12-acre outdoor Museum of Ranch Headquarters, to preserve and exhibit authentic materials of pioneer importance in West Texas from the 1830's to the turn of the century.

Texans have always been big talkers. They have had a lot to talk about. In politics this has led to flamboyant oratory and a procession of Democrats in State legislative and executive government and in Congress. Not from Reconstruction days to 1961 was a Republican elected U.S. Senator; then Texas chose John Tower. However, the State did go Republican in 1928 for Hoover and in 1952 for Eisenhower.

In religion that same verbosity led to the predominance of "rant and rave" Baptist evangelism after the break from Mexico and Catholicism. Most of the first Protestant ministers came into the Red River valley, where Clarksville was the frontier town in the 1830's and 1840's. They were Baptists, Methodists, Presbyterians, and Campbellites. German immigrants brought the Lutheran Church with them. The first Episcopal minister settled on the coast of Matagord. Jews were in the original Stephen Austin colony. Later in the 19th century all the other Protestant sects came in. Religion has played a most important part in Texas in sponsoring colleges and hospitals.

One can go on adding facts, but the quality of distinction of Texas eludes the facts. Americana is made up of facts and events of time and place, but their effects have to be seen and felt in any region. Perhaps because Texas has more of both time and place, there is an atmosphere that has become tangible.

V

SOMETHING of the bigness, the sheer horizon to horizon vistas of forest, coastline, plains, tropical valley, prairie, and the gigantic surprise of mountains along a great river's bend, something of the blend of conquerors, left a psychic pollen to be blown and germinated through the generations. Even the little men who came and who come to Texas felt and feel bigger, taller, as if by instinct of reaction to environment they must measure up to an old tradition.

There seems to be recall even today in the blood of those first sights of pines high as a man could look up, of land to grow more cotton than in all the Old South, of grass for grazing all the cattle a man could herd, of room for men and women who wanted to live close together or miles apart with only a windmill to signal that man was there.

There is still nostalgic music in the names of towns that came on the map, such names as San Augustine, Waxahachie, Corsicana, Waco, Wichita, Mexia, Muleshoe, New Braunfels, San

Marcos, Spur, Uvalde, White Deer, Sweetwater, Presidio, Goodnight, Matador, Pecos, Van Horn. . . . The list could go on for many pages.

Never has man's curiosity, his ingenuity and restless daring been satisfied with crossing continents and oceans. What is above? What is below? Always and everywhere the lure of greater riches of experience, adventure, advantage turn him into a bird, a fish, a gopher. He must fly, swim, dig. In Texas he dug, and as oil and gas came over him he choked and gasped and saw gold— gold that the Conquistadors seeking it never knew was under their horses' feet.

The Indians had known and used surface seepage oil for healing. De Soto had calked his boats with it near Sabine Pass in 1543. But that was long before the century of wheels and pistons when fuel would be fortune.

Few who travel only the routine circuit of the major cities by air or on the more than 65,000 miles of highways are little aware of the regions varied enough to compose the five states which Texas reserved the right by treaty to divide itself into if it wished. Often less than a hundred miles spell the difference in soil and the ways of life which result. A world apart is the "black land" and its north central Texas society of American midwest and eastern influence from the tropical jungle known as the Big Thicket in southeast Texas where the primitive is still present. So too the pine forest land of east Texas where the Old South heritage prevails even in the backwoods area is a far cry indeed from the windswept west of the high plains, the Caprock and Panhandle which knew New England cultural effects in their settlement. Far removed in terrain and spirit and Germanic heritage is also the hill country of south central Texas from the Latin-Americanism of the Rio Grande valley. Still another set of extremes is the 370-miles long coastal stretch of ports, harbors, islands in contrast to the high mountains of the Trans-Pecos which top 8,000 feet in the Chisos of the Big Bend and the Davis and Guadalupe peaks.

Where the main resource is space for everything on two legs or four, it was not at all illogical to locate the NASA headquarters in Texas for the control of outer space exploration. That location, as all the world knows, is adjacent to Houston.

Everyone knows about NASA just as everyone knows and goes to the Astrodome, the Alamo, Six Flags Over Texas, Neiman-Marcus, the Tyler Rose Festival, the Southwestern Exposition and Fat Stock Show Rodeo, the John F. Kennedy assassination site. But the mistake that most visitors (and many residents) make is not getting off the routine tourist track. They need to see at eye level the panorama of cotton, corn, wheat, rice, oats, hay, sorghum, pecan groves, the moving herds of beef and dairy cattle, sheep and goats, the huge flocks of turkeys, all the variegated wealth of Texas.

They need to see the color brilliance of Palo Duro Canyon south of Amarillo, the sociological wonder of Cal Farley's Boys Ranch in the Panhandle, the authentic drama of Albany's annual Fandangle, the fantastic immensity of the Big Bend, the sentinel isolation of McDonald Observatory above mile-high Fort Davis, the winter sanctuaries of Aransas and Rockport and Anahuac Wildlife Refuges, the secluded Elisabet Ney Museum in Austin, studio of one of the most remarkable sculptors and characters in 19th-century art.

They need to see the pine-draped campus of Stephen F. Austin State University in old Nacogdoches, where a main street once followed the winding trail of three centuries ago, El Camino Real, the King's Highway, the trail followed by La Salle in 1685 when it was referred to "as well-beaten a road as that from Paris to Orleans".

They need to see the ante-bellum Excelsior Hotel in Jefferson and the way Jay Gould signed his name in the registry ledger, the man who vowed he would ruin the town as distribution center to the western frontier—and did.

They need to see the oil derrick "Christmas trees" with their holiday lights through East Texas and stop to listen to the throbbing rhythm of the pumps.

They need to see what is left of the rivers after the making of many lakes, the full bloom of cotton and blue-bonnets and Indian paintbrush, the green-gold shimmer of mesquite, the dogwood and, yes, the magnolias, the windmills turning above the cattle grazing, the stars above the wilderness height of Guadalupe, and if possible, the dark blue skyline of a "norther" blowing in.

They need to see the antelope, deer and wild turkey along the highway from Brackettville to Del Rio and to hear the mourning doves in the trees at Uvalde.

They need to see the orange and grapefruit groves in bloom in the great Rio Grande Citrus Valley, mile after mile, origin of the world-famed pink grapefruit.

They need to see the coastline and islands where pirates

once took refuge and where now the snowy egrets and blue herons watch the shrimp boats.

They need to see the ghostly cypress rising from the waters of Caddo Lake in Northeast Texas where the mood lingers from a classic story of love and hate and murder enacted there well over a century ago, the Texas Republic's famous and infamous Robert Potter and the woman who thought she was his wife.

They need to see the moss-hung banks of the Neches River as it drifts into Beaumont where so much of the Spindletop hysteria was absorbed before the advent of today's port industry.

They need to see the curve of the Concho River as it holds together the town of San Angelo, center of America's sheep and wool market.

Such things, and many more, equate the understanding of the complex of Texas just as much as the sight of metropolitan skylines, expressways and runways, or the physique of industry.

In sports Texas has its own unique madness of devotion, and especially is this true in football. When the Matador gallops his black quarterhorse ahead of the Texas Tech team or when Southern Methodist University races its mustang pony Peruna onto the field of week-end battle or the University of Texas parades its prized longhorn Bevo, or the Baylor University bears growl, or the Rice University owl opens and flashes its eyes, the Southwest Conference masses let out cries reminiscent of *Remember the Alamo! Remember Goliad!* at San Jacinto.

In professional football there is the same frontier blood-and-guts support for the Dallas Cowboys and the Houston Oilers. Professional baseball, basketball, hockey, soccer, plus tennis, golf, horsemanship, hunting, fishing, boating, swimming round out the Texans' outdoor loves and skills. It is not by accident that the history of sports in America has been led by so many Texans —Babe Didriksen, Rogers Hornsby, Ben Hogan, Byron Nelson, Wilmer Allison, Doak Walker, Sam Baugh, Bobby Layne, to name only a few.

Statistics, however, are for computers. They serve human society but can never represent it. After all, who can visualize the 276,600 square miles or 177,052,700 acres which are Texas?

In a state of such size where the population is over eleven million of multiple races and national backgrounds, there are inevitable extremes in economic and social levels. Great wealth exists beside great poverty. Yes, there *are* poor Texans, miserably poor. So too a very high degree of culture faces the lowest level of ignorance and illiteracy.

This is the way it is. This is not the way it will remain. Nothing in Texas has ever been static. There is constant progress. There is always a Texas-size tomorrow.

As a poet has expressed it:

TEXAS

The strength of oxen trudging through the wilderness,
The human tide of men advancing with their loves and lives
Into a land whose untamed spirit
  Knew but calls of coyotes in the night,
The swift and silent flash of Indian arrows
Darting after flying herds whose hooves beat out a song
A hundred years ago.

That song was heard;
That promise was fulfilled;
Men saw a vision in the sunset fires
And brought that vision down to earth.
They worked for it and fought for it and died for it,
And as they passed they left behind
A vision new in sunset fires for other men
A hundred years ago.

Gone is that wilderness
But not the spirit whose home it was,
For men still dream and men still build,
And cities are where camp-fires gleamed,
Cities where steel rings true on steel,
And towers rear their gray stone heads
Where soaring engines cleave the sky like playthings
Of these children of a race that vanished
Only to return again inspired by growth to greater growth
A hundred years from now.

PORT ISABEL AND PADRE ISLAND

Picturesque and historic is the lighthouse marking the Queen Isabella Causeway, the southern entry to Padre Island from Port Isabel near the border city of Brownsville.

The 110-mile long island of sand dunes ever shifting in the Gulf wind with their growth of sea oats, Spanish daggers and primroses, nesting place of sea gulls and tropical birds, resting place of driftwood and countless shells from the blue water, offers fishing and beachcombing at their best.

Extending up to Corpus Christi, this long finger of a barrier island, which varies from a few hundred yards to three miles in width, is now a National Seashore and administered by the National Park Service. Once the home of the Karankawa Indian tribe, it came to be called Padre for the Spanish missionary Padre Nicolas Balli, who came in 1800 to attempt conversion of the Indians.

Now Padre Island converts all who come to it for the sheer beauty of nature, the pagan kiss of sea upon sand.

32

THE VALLEY

The people who live along the 36-mile palm-lined highway from Harlingen to Mission refer to it as "the longest Main Street in the World," So it is, though it could also be called Citrus Avenue, for here is a chain of towns and small cities linking the shops, resort facilities and fine homes, fruit packing and canning plants, warehouses and loading platforms, and beyond all the groves of grapefruit, lemon and orange trees that stretch away as far as the eye can see.

This is the heart that pulsates through the lower Rio Grande, the delta fertility of The Valley, bright with sunshine and bougainvillea.

Farthest south of all American cities is Brownsville on the border. Westward are Mercedes, Weslaco, Donna, McAllen, Edinburg—names stamped on myriad crates of fruit and vegetables and on labels of juice cans in the nation's supermarkets.

Here is the state's great garden of riches in the famously mild climate, which normally never freezes and fears only the hurricane—but always survives it.

CORPUS CHRISTI

A bay city always has a beauty all its own and usually a special interest, whether it be Naples or San Francisco or Corpus Christi.

It was the Festival Day of Corpus Christi, as proclaimed by the 13th century Pope Urban IV, when Alvarez Alonzo de Pineda first sailed into the blue water bay in 1519 and gave that name to his discovery.

Other explorers and the gulf coast pirate Jean Lafitte also came into this port and tarried on the two islands that form it, which later were named Padre and Mustang.

Settlement of the mainland began in the late 1830's with ranch headquarters and trading post. General Zachary Taylor brought his troops there in 1845, including young officers such as Robert E. Lee, Ulysses S. Grant, Jefferson Davis, and William T. Sherman. One of the men reported in a letter that the place "contains few women and no ladies".

Less than twenty years later, during the Civil War, the town and port were blockaded by Federal gunboats.

Today all the variegated color of its past has been absorbed into a city whose downtown business district is immediately adjacent to a marine and deep-water port that ranks among the top ten in America. Here, on the city's shore are the three T-shaped piers, one of which is pictured on the opposite page. Dramatically, the skyline of a modern city rises above the yacht basin and ships from all over the world, handling cargoes of cotton, oil, grain, chemicals and fruit.

A convention coliseum, the semi-tropical climate, and the beauty of the shoreline, add up to a very big tourist resort attraction. Nearby, too, is the nation's largest naval air station, headquarters of the U.S. Naval Air Advance Training Command.

The University of Corpus Christi and Del Mar College, fine arts programs and a symphony orchestra, are additional attractions when visitors are not fishing or treasure-hunting on Padre and Mustang Islands.

SEA SPRAY AND SEAFOOD

The hundreds of miles of Texas coastline along the Gulf of Mexico are salty with sea spray and history and all the delicious fruits of the sea.

One of the state's great commercial assets is the enormous quantity and high quality of seafood taken by its fishermen all the way from the Galveston to the Corpus Christi areas. Almost a national supply of shrimp is dredged by the huge nets of the shrimpers who operate in boats such as those from Aransas pictured here.

Crabs and oysters are another profit and gastronomical pleasure. Fishing with bait, both as a business and as a sport, is equally successful. Some fifty varieties of fish are caught, among them sea trout, pompano, flounder, red snapper, Spanish mackerel, which are flown to the leading restaurants of fine cuisine all over America, as well as to the markets that supply the demand of a public with taste for the distinctive in seafood.

THE BISHOP'S PALACE

This showplace on Broadway, in Galveston, suits the dignity of a diocesan see, but it was not designed for a prelate's quarters. Actually a lawyer lived here among the tapestries, thick carpets, finely matched woods, and sparkling chandeliers. Colonel Walter Gresham, a Civil War veteran who later sat in the U.S. House of Representatives, gave his architect, Nicholas J. Clayton, a free hand to express in his home the elegance of his time.

The big circular bay led a fashion; soon owners of more modest rectangular dwellings were adding one. The delicately wrought iron, especially visible in the balconies of the third story, was a gratuitous embellishment. Tall chimneys went with minarets. The furnishings were costly and ornate, but these did not survive. Their quality may be inferred from the woodwork, so typical of its time. White mahogany, red mahogany, satinwood, cherry, walnut and pine formed a rich background, and still persists in these rooms.

The Bishop's Palace illustrates a Texan tendency that still exists—to build substantially with the tools of one's own time. It leads the list of outstanding historic homes—Heidenheimer's Castle, the Trube House, Landes Home, Ashton Villa—for which Galveston is famous.

Galveston, located on an island 30 miles long, 2 miles wide, and 2 miles off the Texas mainland, has grown into one of the most profitable ports on the Gulf, importing sugar and bananas, shipping cotton, grain, sulphur, fuel oils. It competes with the great ports nearby such as Houston, Texas City, Port Arthur, and Beaumont with much the same spirit that made it survive the piracy of Jean Lafitte and the most destructive hurricanes that ever battered the American continent.

The great investments of Galveston are in education, medical facilities and the entertainment of conventions and large-scale tourism. Among the many institutions of importance are the University of Texas Medical Branch and Nursing School, John Sealy Hospital, Galveston Community College, U.S. Public Health Service Hospital, Texas Maritime Academy of A. & M.

Galveston is Galvez-town, so named for the 18th century Count Bernardo de Galvez, Viceroy of Mexico and Spanish Governor of Louisiana, who was known, appropriately for Galveston, as a gourmet of seafood.

40

THE ORANGE GROVES

The whole nation has a stake in the orange groves of Texas. Elder citizens may recall that as long as fifty years ago people in states as far apart as New Jersey and Illinois were sending weekly or monthly payments to land dealers in South Texas to acquire lots on which to raise oranges. Trees would be supplied by growers, and hopeful buyers would look forward five or more years to the time when they might get a crop.

Their dreams have been fulfilled a long time. Their expectations of picking succulent fruit from the trees have been realized. Texas oranges now compete in the markets with the strongly established California and Florida species, and the crop from the area of the Rio Grande is quickly exhausted. Today the trees are sturdy and well-cared for. Many of the original investors not only completed their payments but moved down to live near the orange groves of the Rio Grande.

Only about the weather have they had to make reservations. At long intervals the storms that sweep up from the Gulf of Mexico test the durability of Texas orange trees. The one of recent memory came in September, 1967, and swamped the groves with floods of water, choked irrigation canals with silt, wiped out garden truck and broke down bridges. What is notable is that the planters not only survive, but mend their groves and prosper. This view of the rows of fruit trees that stretch for miles along the roads of Southeastern Texas is proof of their durability.

42

THE FORT AND MISSION OF LA BAHIA

La Bahia is short for a Spanish outpost that began at a bay and ended at a river. It began as a fort, the Presidio Nuestra Senora de Loreto de la Bahia (Fort of Our Lady of Loreta of the Bay), erected in 1722 near the site where La Salle's early fort had stood, as a deterrent to any more foreign incursions. With the soldiers came padres, who worshipped in the little chapel and tried to convert the Indians. But neither padres nor soldiers found the location suitable for their labors, and four years later they established themselves on the Guadalupe River, near today's city of Victoria. In 1749 they moved again, but although this time they settled on the San Antonio River, fort and shrine retained the name of La Bahia.

Both Presidio and Mission have been restored and are now preserved in Goliad State Park. In the chapel of the Presidio is the shrine of Our Lady of Loreta of the Bay. Around Presidio clusters a bloody history of fighting and massacre that began when a group of Americans took the side of Mexican independence and drove the Spaniards out of Presidio. In 1817 a similar force of American irregulars had fifty men killed at the Presidio. In 1821 a force from Mississippi captured the fort. But all of this was merely preliminary to the real encounter that came when the Texans had become powerful enough to challenge the oppressive Mexican government of Santa Anna. Although Santa Anna had sent reinforcements to La Bahia the Texans captured it, and on December 20, 1835, issued the first and unofficial declaration of Texan Independence.

The real tragedy came a few months later, when Santa Anna threw all his forces against the Texans at the Alamo and at Goliad. Colonel James W. Fannin marched out to help the Alamo, failed to get there, and had to surrender to the Mexican General Urrea, who carried out Santa Anna's order to execute all prisoners, including Fannin. Thus March 27, 1836, the Mission fathers lost another battle to savagery, for 342 Texans were massacred that morning. Less than a month later General Sam Houston's army charged to victory at San Jacinto with the cry, *Remember the Alamo! Remember Goliad!*

La Bahia remembers it all.

44

BIG THICKET, A THREATENED WONDERLAND

Sometimes a region of country can be so richly fertile that its people assume their exploitation and vandalism will be remedied by nature indefinitely. Unfortunately this attitude in East Texas vitally endangers one of the most remarkable wilderness areas in the United States—the Big Thicket.

Only 300,000 acres remain of the original three million, and daily violation and destruction go on at an alarming rate. Owned mainly by five lumber companies and open to pipeline installations, it is unprotected and unpreserved by state law. Only Federal conservation can save it as a National Park.

Plant and animal life from three different climate zones come together: magnolia, palmetto palms, cypress; there are some twenty varieties of wild orchids, 300 bird species including the last of the ivory-billed crow-size woodpeckers; bears, panthers, and strange carnivorous plants. Natural scientists call it the last true wilderness. As pictured in this Pine Island Bayou scene, the interior is often of a jungle density called "tight-eye."

Confederate draft-dodgers hid in it. So did and do the moonshiners, famed for a brew more like drambuie in taste than bourbon and of such high potency that a few drinks enable one to see the ghosts of those who entered the Thicket and never found their way out.

North of the Thicket is the Alabama–Coushatta Indian Reservation. South of it are the urban millions of Beaumont and Houston. In it a priceless world of nature fights a losing battle against man. Hopefully control from Washington will rescue and preserve what is left of this wilderness wonder.

SAN JACINTO, SHRINE OF PATRIOTISM

A memorial monument should present historical significance defined through beauty.

Here, by the photographer's art, the San Jacinto Memorial Monument appears in the distance as if framed by gigantic pylons. This simple spire of classic proportions is a giant finger pinpointing the battlefield where, on April 21, 1836, General Sam Houston led his outnumbered Texans to victory over the Mexican army and the capture of their leader, Santa Anna.

On this soil was won revenge for Goliad and the Alamo, independence for Texas, and formation of the Republic of Texas under its Lone Star Flag. The monument, 570 feet, $4\frac{1}{2}$ inches tall, has the Lone Star at its peak. The base holds the San Jacinto Museum of History. The spire is reflected in the long pool at its base, at the end of which is the site where Sam Houston's men camped before the battle. In an inlet from the Houston Ship Canal nearby lies the U.S. Battleship *Texas*, veteran of two World Wars, now flagship of the Texas Navy. Both the monument and the ship are visited annually by thousands of Texans and out-of-state tourists.

48

JEFFERSON, WHERE NOSTALGIA THRIVES

Every spring the question is "Are you going to Jefferson?"

Many people do go and then the little town awakes from the sleep imposed on it by Jay Gould so many decades ago and hums with tourism as the annual pilgrimage brings the history-lover and sightseer to the ante bellum homes and Excelsior House hotel.

Before tycoon Jay Gould uttered his curse, "I'll see grass grow in the streets of Jefferson!" when his railroad plan was not accepted by the city, this was the prosperous river port and distribution center for North and East Texas. The Big Cypress and Caddo Lake were navigable and connected the Red River to the Mississippi. Cargoes and passengers came on side-wheelers from St. Louis and New Orleans to go inland. Memories went back to days of the Republic of Texas, and before. The future was bright with economic promise. Then came Gould and the promise ended as the future rode out on a railroad track by way of Marshall, near enough for Jefferson to hear the train whistle and see the smoke billow above the pine trees.

But for period nostalgia Jefferson holds yesterday for today.

50

HOUSTON, CITY OF SPACE AND ENERGY

Houston, the Space City, is number one in size in Texas. According to an old joke it was said that where the city limits of Los Angeles end, Houston's begin.

A tidewater port on coastal prairie fifty miles inland with a ship channel to the Gulf, Houston handles the third largest ocean tonnage in the United States.

Once briefly the capital of the Republic of Texas, the city has become a citadel of capital with reputedly the highest per capita wealth in the nation.

Manufacturing, industry, banking, distribution and retailing maintain phenomenal growth. The climate is often criticized but not by those aware of the gold in that humidity, as well as the tropical beauty of foliage and flowers that it brings.

Home of the world-famed Astrodome sports area, Houston is equally celebrated as a medical, educational and cultural center. The University of Houston and Rice University are its academic pride. Its museum of Fine Arts was the first in Texas. At the feet of its downtown skyscrapers is the splendid new Civic Center complex of auditoriums for symphonic music, ballet, opera and theater, plus a coliseum and convention halls.

Houston is conscious of both past and future, adjacent as it is to San Jacinto Memorial Battleground and the Manned Spacecraft Center. This gives the metropolis balance. Another asset is nearness to Galveston Island, one of the State's most popular resorts for swimming and fishing, and the tourist attraction of historic homes and buildings flanked by oleander bushes.

Houston has the independence of spirit of the man for whom it was named.

THE ASTRODOME IN HOUSTON

The original idea behind Houston's Astrodome goes back to classical times. Whenever spectators gathered in large numbers to witness contests of endurance and skill, efforts were made to provide seats for the assembly. But at the most famous of ancient amphitheaters, the Roman Coliseum, the topmost benches had poor visibility and all ranks were liable to be swept by winds and drenched by rain. The circus men who boasted of The Big Top as "the greatest," provided a billowing roof, but there still were ridge poles and lateral supports to interfere with a clear view of the proceedings. Only in recent decades has technology removed all the obstacles, and today the Astrodome stands forth as the spectator's ideal, a place brighter than daylight, protected against sun, rain, and vagaries of temperature, where warmth and coolness are provided at will and the human eye has a clear view of more than 600 feet—if it should need to look that far.

The Astrodome is an architectural milestone that gives distinction to the 1960's. Like all big achievements it becomes an example to follow. Already other cities are constructing arenas embodying many of the technical advantages of the Astrodome. Inspiring them is the hope that long lines of spectators will form for baseball, football, all the competitive sports, as in the Harris County Sports Stadium complex. Its immense popularity brings us to an understanding of why the Romans built permanent arenas wherever they settled down. The love of watching competitive play, which permits the spectator to identify himself with the actor, has been an expression of satisfaction through the ages.

TYLER, ROSES AND OIL

Beauty is not what one expects to find in an oil field, but beauty is the distinctive characteristic of the East Texas city of Tyler because of man's development of a gift from the world of nature.

The gift is the rose, and it comes from the very soil under which flows the oil.

Tyler is literally a rose capital, with fields covered with rose bushes that supply half the nation. The annual Rose Festival is a major event for tourists in this city of beautiful homes and gardens. With such a harvest, plus colleges and a symphony orchestra, Tyler has provided a background of gracious living for the transactions of its many oil companies.

In the illustration opposite is a segment of the Municipal Rose Garden, where 27,000 plants put on a spectacular show of 375 varieties of one of nature's finest achievements—the rose.

BLUEBONNETS AND HILL COUNTRY

Texans call it simply the Hill Country, but it became nationally known as LBJ country, the home of former President Lyndon B. Johnson.

A favorite scene is this one of Packsaddle Mountain with the state flower, the bluebonnet, in the foreground and massed along the road. Packsaddle is between Llano and Burnet. Many Indian arrowheads are still to be found in this area.

The Hill Country undulates westward from Austin and San Antonio and the land in between, hills and valleys with six lakes of 700 miles of shoreline— Marble Falls, Inks, Buchanan, Austin, Travis and Lyndon B. Johnson.

Cattle, sheep and goats graze under cedar, mesquite and cypress beside hundreds of springs. The rivers have names sounding strange to the non or new Texan—Sabinal, Frio, Llano, Blanco, Guadalupe, Medina, Pedernales. . . .

The towns are many and old and atmospheric, and near them are dude ranches for the vacationer who prefers a horse to a boat, yesterday instead of today.

BELOW THE DOUBLE DOME

A capital city is always one of special interest, because it exists for a special purpose. When to that is added the main campus of the State's biggest university, the city has an atmosphere that sets it apart even more. Youth and politics are a heady combination.

But still another factor distinguishes Austin: the natural beauty of its setting among the hills and lakes along the Colorado River. The city is split-level with homes perched on cliffs affording panoramic views.

The effect of natural beauty is always a serenity, and this is a rare commodity in cities of today. But Austin has it—a livable quality. As in West Texas, so too in Austin the people stop to look at the sunset, and to watch the mists over the hills that O. Henry once likened to a violet crown.

Because of these attractions the city grows steadily, but the growth does not generate pressure or tension. Big business and important research have an ever-increasing momentum, but Austin keeps its composure and awareness of history. Even when the planes of Bergstrom Air Force Base are in the air, they seem to be marginal to the city, not integral.

The excitement of politics and the collegiate events of University of Texas, St. Edward's University, Houston–Tillotson College, Concordia Lutheran College, Episcopal and Presbyterian Theological Seminaries, and Maryhill College, are all absorbed in the Austin ambiance.

The double dome of the native red granite Capitol—only St. Paul's in London and the Vatican in Rome have domes of such design—the museums and libraries, parks and lakes; the distinctive nightlighting, the relaxed way of life—all add up to a city that is the cultural home of Texas.

LANDSCAPE OF THE COLORADO

The Colorado River, which plays a major part in the drainage system of the Southwest, contributes to the scenic richness of the hill country above Austin. It also gives the people of Austin a place for swimming and boating where the Tom Miller Dam impounds its waters for Lake Austin. There are three miles of shoreline bordered by woods with luxuriant foliage, where public parks increase the opportunities for recreation, with golf courses, bridle paths, riding stables, and shelters for week-end vacations.

There is another duty that the Colorado River performs for Austin, and that is providing its water by means of a great reservoir impounded by the Mansfield Dam. This is called Lake Travis, biggest of the Texas Highland Lakes, for the famous hero of the Alamo, Colonel William B. Travis, and famed for the residential-resort development of Lakeway where all the water sports can be enjoyed.

62

FORT WORTH

To the East Texan, Fort Worth is "where the West begins". This means a big-city atmosphere of friendly informality where there remains the after-glow of a frontier town.

This is where the prairie begins to undulate with hills. This is where the livestock and meat-packing industry held first place before becoming surpassed by the profits of oil and oil well supplies. This is where powerful banks today toss their skyscraper heads like the old longhorns.

This is also where an outstanding Convention Center is combined with a handsome auditorium for the opera, symphony and theater. The new complex adds to the facilities of the Will Rogers Memorial Coliseum and Municipal Auditorium. Easily accessible to the public is the Amon Carter Museum of Western Art, famed for its priceless collection of Remingtons and Russells.

Since the days of Billy Rose the Casa Manana shows have been a most popular attraction, but the excitement of the year comes with the gigantic annual Southwestern Exposition and Fat Stock Show with its original indoor rodeo.

Fort Worth was never a fort. It was a camp site in 1849 for a military guard against the Indians. The cattle trails made it into a town for trade. Its evolution into railroad shipping and ranch financing made it inevitably a city of stability.

BIG D, WITH A BLACK-TIE PERSONALITY

Dallas likes to be called what it usually is—Big D.

Second in size in Texas, it is first in sophistication. Fashion originates in Dallas, notably at Neiman–Marcus. In fact the social whirl here exhausts every women's editor. The city proper embraces several residential municipalities, which bring total population to well over one and a half million.

The city is geared to the demands of a convention center with huge trade exhibit marts, their related facilities, and dozens of social and professional clubs. The annual State Fair calls out the largest gate in the country. Another major event is the Cotton Bowl classic on New Year's Day, when the champion team of the Southwest Conference meets its challenger. City pride focuses on its skyscrapers, its azalea gardens, the new Texas Stadium for the Dallas Cowboys, and the seventh busiest airport in the nation.

Theaters, Community Course, Summer Musicals and Civic Music schedules are maintained. A fall tradition is the Book and Author Luncheon. Art galleries and museums are numerous. Dallas is culture oriented with its symphony orchestra, ballet, Civic Opera and Metropolitan Opera season, even though a modern auditorium is a hope deferred.

Banking, insurance, distribution, retailing, and medical services were among its principal activities until after World War II, when manufacturing became dominant, especially in apparel, foods, electronics, oil well supplies, building materials, and the aircraft industry. Education is accented by multiple degree-granting colleges and universities.

Dallas has a pioneer background dating back to the early 1840's, but it never was a frontier town. It grew into a city with precision and purpose. It is Big D with a black-tie personality to match.

66

SAN ANTONIO AND THE PASEO DEL RIO

The word forever associated with San Antonio is charm. Charm is not an easy word to define. Neither is San Antonio. Both are an experience of personality and atmosphere.

San Antonio is Texas with the full flavor of the old days when Texas was Spain and Mexico. From the Alamo and the other four old missions comes a mood of Catholic history still strong enough to embrace a modern city. It is this presence of yesterday in today that brings the tourist, and brings him back: charm.

Is it the river? The little San Antonio River winds its picturesque way fifteen miles, crossing six miles of city streets, a river spanned by bridges and edged with landscaped walkways, restaurants and art shops of the Paseo del Rio, pictured on the opposite page. The Indians once had a word for this river centuries ago when only a settlement was here; the word meant "drunk old man going home at night."

So, too, the river winds through the largest of all metropolitan parks, Brackenridge Park, originally a grant of land from the King of Spain over two centuries ago.

Then there is the military mood emanating from Fort Sam Houston, headquarters of the Fourth U.S. Army, and four great Air Force bases.

Fine parochial schools and colleges and Trinity University offer outstanding educational variety, and the San Antonio Symphony Orchestra, annual Opera Festival, Little Theater in San Pedro Playhouse, the permanent interest of the site of the 1968 Hemisfair, all add cultural zest to a city of new big business, very old history and natural sunlit beauty.

But the tempo was set long ago in the missions, so that there is a soft mellowing of time to relax the nerves in San Antonio and bring to mind words like *mañana* and *fiesta* or, in English, charm.

In San Antonio one hears the whisper of heroic ghosts—Travis, Bowie, Crockett, Bonham. . . .

68

THE ALAMO

Actually the Alamo was not a mission but a chapel attached to the original mission San Antonio de Valero which, with the presidio San Antonio de Bexar, was the start of San Antonio in 1718, when it was desirable to have a halfway post between Mexico and the East Texas missions. The Alamo itself was built *circa* 1754. Its use as a chapel ceased in 1793.

Today the death of 187 men in battle is a small figure. Their eternal distinction is the way they died—that they chose to fight to their last breath to free Texas from the oppression of a tyrant.

Those 187 men asked no questions. They knew the answer as their commander William Barret Travis phrased it in three words "Victory or Death!" A recent Poet Laureate of Texas, Dr. Jenny Lind Porter, adapted the famous Travis farewell letter into poetic form:

February 24, 1836

"People of Texas and Americans,
My fellow citizens throughout the land,
My dear compatriots—I am besieged!
It seems a thousand, and it may be more
Of Santa Anna's Mexicans who throng
About the streets and plazas of the town.
I have sustained continual cannonade
Twenty-four hours, losing not a man.
How long may it be so? The enemy cries,
'Surrender at discretion!'—otherwise
They'll take the fortress, put us to the sword.
A single shot has answered their demand,
And our flag answers proudly on the walls,
And I say Never! to the word retreat,
Never surrender! calling still on you,
On you, my kinsmen, if you now hold dear
The name of liberty, if you can hear
The name of conscience and the name of faith,
By all the character of patriot love,
Come to us, help us, brethren, in our need.
The enemy increases, day by day,
Three or four thousand gather in a week,
But hearing never from you, will I stand
Sustained, sustaining, dying like a man
Who as a soldier could not soon forget
What is due honor, in the face of death,
What is due country with a dying breath,
    And I am one who always pays his debt.
    Victory or Death!"

WILLIAM BARRET TRAVIS

MISSION SAN JOSE

San José has long been called Queen of the Missions in Texas. The man responsible for its concept, location and beauty was Fray Antonio Margil de Jesus of the College of Zacatecas.

The pioneer priest, who called himself "la misma nada" (the same nobody) and who also compiled a dictionary of many Indian dialects, founded and named the Mission San José y San Miguel de Aguayo in 1720 to honor the Governor of Coshuila and Texas at that time.

Priests, Indians and soldiers built San José, and they built it well, for years of work went into the stone walls, arches, carving and sculpture, the tower and dome and forever photographed "rose window." This is the window that was the work of a Spanish sculptor related to the architect of the Alhambra, and took five years to complete. It also holds the legend of the artist's love for a girl named Rosa.

Now San José Mission is a State Park and a National Monument, as it deserves to be.

72

MISSION CONCEPCION

Mission Nuestra Señora de la Purisma Concepcion was built in East Texas near the Angelina River in the summer of 1716. Supposedly it was for the conversion and teaching of the Hasani Indians. Actually it was another outpost for Spain to prevent French expansion into Texas.

When the threat disappeared and military support was withdrawn, the padres asked and were granted permission to transfer the mission to San Antonio. The move was made in 1731, and the building that stands there today is the best preserved of any of the historic missions in Texas.

Facing west with twin towers and Moorish dome, the adobe walls are 45 inches thick. The faded frescoes can still be seen.

Until the turn of the century Concepcion was still in use for priestly training and teaching. Then an orphanage and seminary were added to the mission grounds. And so the past lived on.

KILGORE, WHERE THE TREES WERE DERRICKS

The smell of oil is sweet to the people in Kilgore, and the sight of oil derricks in clusters like groves of giant trees is scenic to their visitors, for in this smell and sight is the success story of fabulous wealth for man and his industrial society.

The man-made forest of derricks, as pictured on the opposite page, has now been cleared, but both history and many personal memories record it as symbol of a fantastic era.

It was near Kilgore just after Christmas, 1930, that a gusher blew in a couple of months after C. M. (Dad) Joiner had struck oil in East Texas. No geologist had considered this an oil potential, but it proved to be one of the great oil discoveries in America.

Today the boom town of Kilgore has matured into a city more likely to express pride in its native son Van Cliburn, or the precision performing Rangerettes of Kilgore College, than in the story of its oil.

Nearby is Longview, the city that also mastered the technique of turning an oil boom into aggressive and progressive stability, for Longview manufactures almost everything from a can of beer to the heaviest machinery. In fact the "long view" origin of its name in 1870 is still operative today, with the prospect of Sabine River navigation to the Gulf as a vision of more good fortune to come.

LUBBOCK, HEART OF AGRIBUSINESS
Pictured here is a scene from the Texas Technological University at Lubbock.

The city stands tall at over 3,200 ft. altitude on the Caprock of West Texas. A dynamic city of phenomenal speed in growth, it centralizes an area that produces half of the State's cotton and leads the world in production of cotton seed oil and grain sorghum for feed. Wheat production is also very high, some 17 million bushels a year. All this on the plains that once were cattlemen's kingdom; now the kingdom is divided and the wealth is all the greater.

The hub of this agribusiness, as they call it, is a city able to play host to many conventions, with a Municipal Coliseum and Auditorium able to accomodate over 10,000.

Lubbock is geared to the arts, especially sculpture and pictorial art, symphonic music and the theater. Home of Texas Tech, there is special pride in the outstanding West Texas Museum on that campus and leadership in research for arid and semi-arid lands.

Shops of high fashion have not eliminated the western informality and spirit characteristic of Lubbock. Even the massive 1970 tornado disaster was taken in stride. People simply went to work rebuilding what they had built— together.

78

AMARILLO AND PALO DURO CANYON

At over 3,600 ft. altitude Amarillo is the major Panhandle city and "helium capital", which has turned to irony the fact that at one time Texas considered the area of so little value that the state offered to exchange over three million acres in this northwest region in order to pay for building the capitol at Austin. That would make the government building worth just about its weight in gold at present land values here. Amarillo looks out over its many satellite towns such as Borger, Pampa, Dumas, Hereford, which are a complex of oil, petro-chemistry, industry, agriculture and ranching. Nearby is the beauty of Lake Meredith, the spacious West Texas State University campus at Canyon with its fascinating Panhandle—Plains Historical Museum. Here visitors enjoy horseback rides amid the scenic splendor of Palo Duro Canyon State Park, where an exciting pageant of area history is expertly staged every summer in a natural canyon amphitheater between high colorful cliffs. In that canyon was Col. Charles Goodnight's ranch, from which he blazed cattle trails to Colorado and Kansas.

Amarillo is thoroughly metropolitan today with its own culture of Civic Center, Amarillo College, symphony and theater, and hub of widely diversified business interest of old stability and new expansion.

Most valuable from the human standpoint is Cal Farley's Boys Ranch on the site of Old Tascosa where disadvantaged and disturbed boyhood is rehabili-tated and directed into the high quality of western manhood and solid citizenry conceived by its founder Cal Farley and continued now by his successors.

IN THE PANHANDLE

Since man began to ranch and then to farm the great Panhandle of west Texas, the windmill has always been the most distinctive silhouette on the horizon. Its tall gaunt frame, at first made of wood and then later of steel, stands symbolic of two things: life because of water, and human habitation. In the old days men climbed up its high structure to hang a lantern to guide riders home at night.

Something of that historic drama of the windmill in the vast solitude and isolation of the high plains has inspired some of the best scenic work of southwestern artists such as Peter Hurd, John Meigs and many others.

Open space and violent extremes of heat and cold made and kept the big country a constant challenge to men for their cattle and crops. Enormous feeding lots were developed to fatten thousands of cattle from the bounty of grain sorghum for the huge auctions and market.

This century added another silhouette to the Panhandle scene. Like the windmill, it too was first of wood and then of steel—the oil derrick. With it came men very different from the ranchers and farmers. But all of them, from cowboy to driller, are vital parts of the windswept pattern of the Panhandle.

ROUND 'EM UP—HEAD 'EM OUT!

Unlike many Americans in other parts of the nation, Texans have no fear of concrete covering the land. Even the cities that have converted farms into urban sub-divisions are aware that they are only on the fringe of a vast open country that is the source of Texas livestock wealth, especially cattle.

In West Texas, where the counties measure size by square miles instead of acres, stretch some of the most productive cattle ranges in America. Even in East Texas the trend is from farming to ranching.

There are Brahman, Black Angus, Brangus, Santa Gertrudis, Charolais . . . but the most popular breed remains the White-face Hereford. They find good pasture, but often now they are driven into feed-lots for additional fattening of their beef before shipping to market.

There are fewer horses on the range now than there used to be, for the cowboy is as often in a jeep or pick-up as on a pony, but the stock in the herds, through expert breeding and selection, is still the same old glory of Texas ranching—and so is the traditional cry "Round 'em up—head 'em out!"

LAMB CHOPS AND WOOL

Despite an equally old history of great interest, books about Texas sheep and goats are scarce and rare, whereas those about cattle can fill a library.

Sheep came into Texas with the Spanish missions and became the native churros of the Mexican herders. The Stephen F. Austin colonist brought in Merinos from the northeast and mid-Mississippi Valley. German and English immigrants settled with their own breeds. But it was a young New Orleans newspaperman, George W. Kendall, who came as reporter to the Republic of Texas and went on the ill-fated Santa Fe Expedition, who brought sheep from Mexico, Vermont, France, Scotland and England into the hill country he selected near New Braunfels as ideal for sheep ranching. Indian raids, natural hazards, and the hostility of cattle ranchers and cowboys were constant threats, but with vigilance the flocks increased into thousands of head.

During the Civil War the Confederacy sorely needed wool for blankets and clothing, but their mills were in Georgia and Virginia and transportation was slow from Texas. Nor did the Mexican herders care to be paid in Confederate currency.

After the Civil War the wool business boomed. In 1866 $2,000,000 worth was shipped from Galveston alone. The famed King Ranch counteracted the depression in beef by turning to sheep. Other leaders who pioneered were the Callahans, Captain Charles Schreiner, Casper Real, and Herman Stieler and his sons, who diversified with Angora goats.

Of special interest were Karl von Schauer, who drove 3,000 sheep from California into West Texas, a three year's trip, and Arthur Anderson of the Hat A Ranch, who trailed his sheep for two years from California to Salt Lake and through Colorado to Texas.

Out of this colorful past, the present prime position of Texas in wool, lamb and mohair production has evolved for America.

SANTA ELENA CANYON IN BIG BEND

Big Bend is the small name for one of the world's most immense landscapes.

Good highway entrances and exits, fine lodging and campsites are the only concessions to so-called civilization in this comparatively new National Park. All the rest is as the elemental forces of nature created it,—the mighty Chisos Mountains and 788,682 acres of land held in the great curving arm of the Rio Grande, land strewn with cacti and over 2,000 varieties of plant life that flower into purple, yellow, red and green patterns of beauty framed in serene solitude.

Here the mule deer and the pronghorn antelope follow trails of the ancient dinosaur, and man follows, too, now on horseback or on foot, quiet with respect and awe for what his long unused senses absorb.

At the precipice edge of dramatic canyons he stares in cathedral silence at the cliffs of Santa Elena, Mariscal, Bouquillas and the fantastic shapes designed by the same mystery of creation which formed himself and brings him to this rendezvous.

IN THE VAST SOUTHWESTERN MOUNTAINS

Only the horseman, gazing out over the breath-taking panorama of the Texas mountain country knows the tremendous uplifting effect this vista has on the human spirit. The horse is at home here and so is man.

Few people think of Texas as mountainous. They don't know until they head south-westward into the vast solitude guarded by the great cactus-crowned peaks of the Davis and Chisos Mountains and Big Bend National Park, where the Colorado-born Rio Grande has cut its southward swing through a series of canyons between stark cliffs nearly 2,000 ft. deep.

The names roll on the tongue softly—Santa Elena, Mariscal, Boquillas. But their reality is rugged immensity and an effect of flame burned into stone. People have said that only Beethoven could have expressed what is to be seen and felt here. Certainly it cannot be done in words, though once a Mexican vaquero of another century tried to tell what he found:

> You ride south from Fort Davis
> Where the rainbow waits for the rain,
> Where the river is kept in a stone box
> And the water runs uphill
> And the mountains tower into the sky
> Except at night when they disappear
> To visit other mountains
> . . . . . Quien sabe?

Who knows indeed? Only this—that one must go there, and having gone, return many times.

OUR NEWEST NATIONAL PARK

Highest of all the mountains in Texas are the Guadalupes, and the Guadalupe Mountains National Park has been created by the Federal Government to provide new bases for both recreation and study. As yet it remains in perfect wilderness purity, and this picture of McKittrick Canyon, with the deer in the background, is one of the few available, for entrance into the Guadalupes is only by horseback or muleback and only with guides. In the future when the public can visit here, it will not find paths worn smooth by generations of human travel, but will be on trails known only to the deer and his redskin brother.

Travelers on the old Butterfield Stagecoach used to look at this great mountain area as they skirted it. So too the modern motorists driving between Carlsbad Caverns and El Paso. In Texas the nearest town is Van Horn, some 60 miles south.

These towering mountains of wilderness with peaks just under 9,000 ft. knife into Texas from New Mexico. Former Secretary of the Interior Stewart Udall described this new Park as "the most beautiful and diversified scenery in the southwestern United States."

According to the great Chief Geronimo, the world's richest gold mines lay hidden in the Guadalupes, flung there by a god angry with man.

THE GATE TO THE NORTH

On May 4, 1598, Juan de Onate, an explorer in the employ of King Philip II of Spain, came to a crossing of the Rio Grande, looked at the mountains to south, west, and north, and called it El Paso del Norte, the Pass of the North. So it was, as the Pueblo Indians already knew.

The Pass it remains, El Paso, the city farthest west in Texas, the largest port of entry from Mexico into the United States. Nestled between river and mountains at over 3,700 ft. altitude, the city of the Sun Bowl has an approach from the east that signals the excitement of change from one part of the continent to another as time goes back an hour. Texas novelist William Humphrey said it memorably: one becomes younger going westward.

El Paso and Juarez look across the river at each other for friendly mutual profit as the tourists go back and forth across the International Bridges. Copper and other crude ores are shipped into El Paso from northern Mexico, New Mexico, Arizona and Colorado. In addition to those smelters are the oil and gas refineries. On land once desert everything grew with irrigation—fine grade cotton, vegetables, pecan and pear trees, chile peppers of special potency, alfalfa for the cattle ranches and feeding lots.

Its very isolation from the rest of Texas had effect on El Paso. It was little interested in the Texas Revolution. It was more concerned with the Butterfield Stage Line, which raced there from Missouri to California, and in later years the battle between the Southern Pacific and the Texas and Pacific Railroads to get first to the Pass.

Now interest focuses on the University of Texas at El Paso—formerly Texas Western—the new Civic and Convention Center, and as always, that biggest of all military posts—the million acres of Fort Bliss.

High above El Paso on the summit of Sierra de Cristo Rey, 4,576 ft., is the 30-foot statue of Christ made of Texas sandstone on a 12-foot base, an old and treasured landmark.

94